Coloured Handprints

ACKNOWLEDGEMENTS

Grateful acknowledgement is made to the editors of the following in which a number of these translations, or versions of them, originally appeared:

Hayden's Ferry Review, The Wolf, Two Lines, The Construction Magazine, Plume, Second Genesis. An Anthology of Contemporary World Poetry (A.R.A.W.LII Publishing), *World Poetry Almanac* and lyrikline.org.

Coloured Handprints

20 GERMAN-LANGUAGE POETS

Edited by Anatoly Kudryavitsky

Translated from the German by
Anatoly Kudryavitsky and Yulia Kudryavitskaya

DEDALUS PRESS
DUBLIN, IRELAND

First published in 2015 by
The Dedalus Press
13 Moyclare Road
Baldoyle
Dublin 13
Ireland

www.dedaluspress.com

ISBN 978 1 910251 11 9

Dedalus Press titles are represented in the UK by
Central Books, 99 Wallis Road, London E9 5LN
and in North America by Syracuse University Press, Inc.,
621 Skytop Road, Suite 110, Syracuse, New York 13244.

Cover image:Copyright © Vasyl Duda | Dreamstime.com

The translation of this work was supported by a grant from the Goethe-
Institut which is funded by the German Ministry of Foreign Affairs.
The translation is also supported by a grant from Bundeskanzleramt
Österreich, the Federal Ministry of Art and Culture, Austria.

The Dedalus Press receives financial assistance from
The Arts Council / An Chomhairle Ealaíon

GOETHE INSTITUT   BUNDESKANZLERAMT ▪ ÖSTERREICH   the arts council / chomhairle ealaíon   funding literature artscouncil.ie

Contents

Anton G. Leinter. Introduction:
Coloured Handprints – in Black on White

⌐

INTRODUCTION

Coloured Handprints – in Black on White

IF YOU ASK young people in Germany (or in Ireland, where things are almost certainly no different) what they want from life, most will say they want to have an adventure. Adventures were always expeditions into the unknown, out of the normal environment into a fascinating venture. Even the medieval singer who travelled into the wide world would bring home for his beloved a song of his "Âventiure" describing his perilous journey into lands unknown.

Today an adventure can be booked on the Internet, with insurance coverage and an all-inclusive package – and, of course, not without the necessary outdoor clothing being provided. But does one really have to travel around the world to experience something exciting? One of the few remaining adventures of today may have to do with poetry, e.g. listening to what a current singer has to report of his "Âventiuren". An anthology that attempts an overview of contemporary German poetry, therefore, is truly an account of an expedition into the unknown, because contemporary German-language poetry is rooted in a difficult terrain.

The ground prepared by the foremost minstrel Walther von der Vogelweide, ploughed by the classics like Goethe and Schiller, and sowed by the pioneers of Modernism, Brecht and Gottfried Benn, was then, after the catastrophe of World War II, dotted with mines. As a result, it is not particularly easy to till. The verdict of the impossibility of "writing a poem after Auschwitz" still hovers over the poets of today. Those who tried anyway had to first engage in a historical and political house-cleaning before they could again deal with metre and metaphor. However at the post-war reconstruction stage the need for metaphorical expressions apparently became so strong that German-language poets wished to excel above all in making their lyrical works as hermetic as possible. Only with the historically significant bringing down of the Berlin Wall and the reunification of East and West Germany the long-stretched era of German post-war poetry finally ended. And with it ended the suppression of free movement and information exchange, as well as the necessity of using Aesopian language.

The present volume returns from its "Âventiure", its expedition to the site of contemporary German-language poetry, having garnered a great deal. In a limited space, it gathers together a polyphonic choir of contemporary poets. From A (Michael) Augustin to Z (Eva) Zeller, the important representatives of German-language literature are here given voice. The youngest among them is Anna Rabe (born in 1986), whereas Peter Turrini, born in 1944, could still feel the consequences of the post-war period when he first sharpened his poetic pencil. There are many excellent and award-winning poets among them, such as the Hamburg-born Jan Wagner, Ludwig Fels from Franconia, or Nora Bossong, originally from Bremen. Fels is now living in Vienna, Wagner and Bossong in Berlin, as is Uwe Kolbe, who documented in his biography the German-German problem, as did the Dresden-born poet Durs Grünbein, whose work has been much praised by literary critics ever since the 1990s.

The topics of the poems included in *Coloured Handprints* range from the generation gap to the financial crisis to existential questions on the future of the planet. While Michael Augustin, employing his distinctive "real-poetic" language and, without anger, takes a look back at the classic poetry and is prescribed a poem by Dr. Benn, Ludwig Fels ponders over "the sheet of paper [...] fully covered with the nothingness of today." Ulla Hahn gives an account of somebody's love-life: "We're so divided that it keeps us together." And Uwe Kolbe acknowledges the following:

"Fathers never die, we hear from time immemorial. As for sons, they rarely live."

Remarkably, despite all the differences in the language, the style and the tone of the "narrative", they all share a very realistic vision of the world. Everything is expressed in no uncertain terms, and the poets give us a clear account of their observations. And so words like "stock index" may end up in one of their verses, as was the case with a Durs Grünbein poem. This adds a bitterly ironic note: "The gold of humanism / Decays solemnly in archives and banks."

Poems show once again that in a time of confusion they can be considered as landmarks. Also, when the old values seem to fade on the horizon, a single verse may succeed in sharpening our view and offering a new perspective, as Jan Wagner asserts in these lines: "in the distance two windmills were drilling / a test borehole in the sky; / god held his breath."

Many years ago the following line from a verse by the great Argentinean poet Roberto Juarroz (1925–1995) became my personal credo: "A poem saves the day." German contemporary poets certainly don't believe that their verses can save the world in an instant. But if at least one of these poems, which now come before the reader's eyes, is able to save their day, the world is not completely lost!

Anton G. Leitner
Wessling, January 2015
Translated from the German by Anatoly Kudryavitsky

Anton G. Leitner is the editor of "Das Gedicht", a magazine of German-language poetry.

Farbige Handabdrücke

Coloured Handprints

Rezept

Doktor Benn
verschreibt ein Gedicht.

Es schmeckt bitter.
Es brennt auf der Zunge.
Es hat einen Nachgeschmack.

Jemand sagt: Es hilft.
Einer fragt: Gegen was.

Michael Augustin (GERMANY)

Michael Augustin was born in Lübeck, Germany, in 1953. A poet, translator and radio commentator, he works for Radio Bremen, where he presents a poetry program and is editor of the weekly documentary. He is the author of a number of poetry books, dramas and short stories, including *A Little Stir* and *Perfect Happiness*. His work has been translated into English, Italian, Polish, Irish and Dutch. He has translated into German works by Roger McGough, Adrian Mitchell and Raymond Carver, among others. He was the recipient of the Friedrich Hebbel and the Kurt Magnus awards. In 2003, he was writer-in-residence at Dickinson College (USA).

Prescription

Doctor Benn
prescribes a poem.

It tastes bitter.
It burns the tongue.
It leaves an aftertaste.

Somebody says: "It helps."
Someone else asks: "Against what?"

Ortsgespräch Lübeck

Gestern Abend
ruft Thomas Mann an.

Was will der denn,
denk ich,
geben einfach
keine Ruh,
die Toten.

Hat sich aber
nur verwählt.

Das ist schön

Sich vorstellen,
wie erst Schiller und dann Goethe
seinen Mund auftut
und die ganze Bagage im Zimmer
sich stillschweigend einig ist:

Diese zwei Männer
sprechen alles andere,
aber mit Sicherheit nicht
die Sprache von Schiller und Goethe.

Local Call, Lübeck

Last night
I got a call from Thomas Mann.

"What does he want?"
I thought.
The dead,
they won't
leave you alone.

But it was just
a misdial.

This is Nice

Imagine
Schiller and then Goethe
open their mouths
and all the rabble in the room
tacitly agree that

these two men
speak anything
but the language
of Schiller and Goethe.

Das ist nicht schön

Seit acht Uhr früh
nichts als Gedichte gelesen.

Siebzehn Stunden lang
nichts als Gedichte.

Davon kann man
verrückt werden,
sagst du.

Und ich weiß,
daß du weißt,
wovon du redest.

Der junge Dichter schreibt zurück an R.

Spät kommt mein Dank für Ihren liebenswerten Brief,
der mich erst jetzt erreicht, nach einer halben Ewigkeit.
Das Dichten, wissen Sie, hab' ich inzwischen aufgegeben
und arbeite als Koch. Wenn Sie mal in der Gegend sind,
dann schaun Sie bitte bei uns rein!

P.S.
Von meinen Wildpastetchen sagt man, sie seien ein Gedicht.

This isn't Nice

From 8 a.m.
nothing but reading poetry.

For seventeen long hours
nothing but poems.

This
can drive a person crazy,
you say.

And I know
that you know
what you're talking about.

The Young Poet Writes Back to R.

Please accept my belated gratitude for your lovely letter
that has just reached me, after half an eternity.
I must confess that I've abandoned my poetic endeavours
and now work as a chef. If you ever come this way,
you are most welcome to pay us a visit.

P.S.
They say my meat pie is pure poetry!

Ach Europa,

auch nur dieses kleine, gerüttelte Wiesending, Königstochter
mit einer panischen Angst vor Stieren, wer nimmt ihr das übel
nach all dem. Kriege hatte sie wie andere Leute Erkältungen.
Eine Schürze voller Länder über die Ebene geschüttelt, Babel
an jedem Grashalm errichtet, Verwaltungschaos drapiert in
Brüsseler Spitze. Ein Panoptikum aus Irren und Ehrenbürgern,
Bagatellen und bösen Geistern. Die Sumpfdotterblume wäre
die sichere Wahl, doch irgendetwas liegt uns an ihr, Europa,
dieser verschreckten Zwergin am Ende der Welt. Wir muntern
sie auf und beteuern, dass es einmal gut ausgeht mit ihr.

Nora Bossong (GERMANY)

Nora Bossong was born in 1982 in Bremen, and now lives in Berlin. She studied literature at the German Institute for Literature, and philosophy, culturology and comparative literature at the Humboldt University of Berlin, the University of Potsdam, and the Sapienza University of Rome. She has published three novels and two collections of poems, the latest being *Summer in Front of the Walls* (2011). Her poetry and prose appeared in many literary journals and have been widely anthologised. She received the Berliner Kunstpreis, awarded to her by the Academy of Arts, Berlin in 2011.

Ah, Europa

She belongs in these narrow, unquiet meadows, a king's
    daughter
with an irrational fear of bulls. Who can blame her
after all that has happened? She suffered from wars as people
suffer from colds. Her apron is full of windfall countries from
    the plain;
Babel built upon every blade of grass, administrative chaos
    draped in
Brussels lace. Lunatics and dignitaries she puts on display,
gabbers and evil minds. The marsh marigold would be
the safe choice, but we like something about her,
Europa, a frightened dwarf at the end of the world. We
    encourage her
and assume that one day she'll come good.

Rolandslied

Und gingen wir durch meine Mutterstadt
fast lautlos, sprach er nichts, als bliebe es so
ungesagt und lag in diesem Sommertag
ein heißes Flustern, gab uns kein Baum,
kein Tunnel Schatten, ließ meine Hand von
seiner Hufte ab und fragte er mich nach
des Laudons Grab - ich weiß nicht, glaub,
er wollte nicht mehr weiter,
mein Vater.

Geweihe

Das Spiel ist abgebrochen. Wie sollen wir
jetzt noch an Marchen glauben? Die Aste
splittern nachts nicht mehr, kein Wild,
das durch die Walder zieht und das Gewitter
lost sich in Fliegenschwarmen auf. Gleichwohl,
es bleibt dabei: Das Jucken unter unsern Fußen
ist kein Tannenrest, kein Nesselblatt, wir folgen noch
dem Dreierschritt, den sieben Bergen und auch
dem Rehkitz Bruderchen und seiner Liebsten.
Erzahl mir die Geweihe an die Wand, erzahl mir
Nadeln in die Fliegen. Im rechten Moment
vergaßen wir zu stolpern.
Schneewittchen schlaft.

Song of Roland

As we went through my home town
almost silently, he said nothing, as though everything
had to remain unsaid, hot whisper
lingering on that summer day,
no tree cast a shadow, no tunnel,
he removed my hand from
his hip and inquired about the location
of von Laudon's grave – I guess, he
no longer wanted to go farther,
my father.

Antlers

The game has been abandoned. How can we
still believe in fairy-tales? The branches
no longer creak at night, deer no longer
run through the woods, and the storm
dissolves in swarms of flies. Still,
it doesn't go away, the foot itch, and it's not
because of prickly roots or stinging nettles. We keep
following the three roads hurrying past the seven hills
after Brother Fawn and his sweetheart.
Tell me about antlers on the wall, tell me
about flies mounted on pins. At the critical moment
we forgot to stumble.
Snow White is sleeping.

Rattenfänger

Zwei Jungen traf ich
unterm Bruckenbogen nachts,
die pinkelten den Pfosten an und
sagten, dass sie sieben seien
sagten, dass sie Lause hatten.
Sie lachten uber mich, als ich
es glauben wollte. Nichts zu holen
außer Lause, verriet der Kleinere.
Er zeigte aufs Gebusch und trat
mir auf den Spann. Ich hatt mich gern
in ihn verliebt, so billig war
in jener Nacht sonst nichts mehr
zu erleben. Der Große fragte, ob es stimmt,
dass auch das Tier allein
nicht sterben kann. Es war
zu spat fur Jungen unter dieser Brucke.

Maria ad Naves

Schneewittchen liegt hier als alter Mann
im Glassarg, das Stück Obst aus Metall.
Ein Schlaf, der selbst Monarchinnen entsetzt,
auch Mary. Ach Mary!
Äpfel glitten dir aus der Hand,
ausgerutscht bist du auf Spiegelbildern,
erstickt an Versen. Hier bleibt zurück:
die kernlose Frucht, das Wachsgesicht,

Ratcatcher

While walking at night, I met two boys
under a bridge.
They peed against the posts; they said
they were seven and then
that they had lice.
They laughed at me, thinking I
was starting to believe them. "There's nothing
to be found here but lice," the younger boy muttered.
He pointed to the shrubs, and stepped
on my foot. I would have liked to
become fond of him, as there were
no other experiences coming cheap
that night. The older boy asked
if it was true that animals, like us,
don't like to die alone. It was too late for those boys
to be out under the bridge.

Maria ad Naves

(The Papal Basilica of Santa Maria Maggiore*)

Snow White rests here as an old man
in a glass coffin, a fruit made of metal.
A sleep that shocked even monarchs,
including Mary Queen of Scots. Oh, Mary!
Apples you let slip from your hand, and you yourself
slipped into reflections in the mirror,
choked on verse. What lingers here are
the seedless fruit, the waxen face,

am Treppenrand die Bettlerin,
sie nennt sich selbst Maria die Große,
gleichgültig alltäglich verfällt sie,
das uralte Mädchen, Mauerblümchen.

the beggar woman at the foot of the stairs,
she who called herself Mary the Great and now
expires daily, indifferently,
an ancient girl, a wallflower.

* *The burial place of St. Pius V.*

lüstern

wenn ich den luster in der oper sehe
möchte ich turnen wie ein affe oder
es herrn tarzan gleichmachen bewegung
soll endorphine freisetzen jeden freitag
sind meine arme zu kurz für ein stummeltier
stammel ich und hänge von der decke
ein zappler seiner beine im luftschloss
plumpst mir der einfall auf den kopf

Manfred Chobot (AUSTRIA)

Manfred Chobot was born in 1947 in Vienna, where he later studied psychology and culturology. Since 1970 he has been working as a full-time writer, and has published volumes of poetry, essays, memoirs, and criticism. His latest poetry collection is *gefallen gefällt* (2012). He has been the Austrian editor of the *Das Gedicht* magazine. Chobot is the author of some fifty plays staged in Austria and Germany, and also broadcast on radio. In 2003, he was awarded an honorary doctorate of literature of the WAAC (The World Academy of Arts and Culture).

Lustres

when I see the chandelier in the Opera House
I want to do gymnastics like an ape or imitate
Lord Tarzan every Friday I make the same
movements that release my endorphins
my arms aren't long enough for a short-limbed animal
I stammer and hang from the ceiling
wriggling my legs in my castle in the air
knocking a stupid idea into my head

"parfum-orgie"

an deinem ohr
    & deiner wange
von der schulter abwärts
    ein geruch
verführt dein körper
    kein käufliches parfum
wie mandeln oder nüsse
    eine prise erdbeeren
vermischt sich vanille mit
    cognac und pfefferoni
leicht geräuchert durch
    paprika und chili
von ingwer eine spur
    & ich suche nach namen
essenzen wie hyazinthen
    magnolien oder hibiskus
verkrümmen sich die nasen
    sämtlicher parfümeure
& schnuppern sich wund
    an oleander und flieder
um deinen duft in einem
    flakon zu bannen
bleibt mir erspart
    den dunst zu benennen
mit dem dein körper
    mich atmen lässt

Interplay of Fragrances

in your ear
   & on your cheek
down from your shoulders
   an odour
takes over your body
   not a cheap perfume
like almonds or nuts
   a handful of strawberries
vanilla mixed with
   cognac and pepperoni
lightly smoked
   with paprika and chilli
and a trace of ginger
   & I'm looking for names
for essences like hyacinth
   magnolia and hibiscus
that tease the noses
   of all perfumers
make them contorted and sore
   sniffing lilac and oleander
to capture your fragrance
   in a bottle
this spares me
   identifying the scent
that your body
   leaves for me to inhale

nachtgedicht

ich lasse mich fallen
in die sprache der nacht
schier endlos berauscht
von der ruhigen finsternis
gelebt und angeschafft
gehört das bett tagträumern
um übernächtig zu übernachten
spricht die nacht tatsächlich
sobald der tag beginnt
    in der nacht

revolution

permanente veränderung ist ausgerufen
zwischen dir und mir
täglich aufs neue
die revolution durchführen
um nicht zu erstarren in routinierter gewöhnung
den zustand prüfen
der abhängigkeit
meine gefühle für dich erneuern
lieber einen gespaltenen schädel riskieren
wie trotzki dereinst
für die theorie

bin ich cäsar der
neue provinzen
für die krone unterwirft ein weltreich aufs spiel setzt

MANFRED CHOBOT

A Night Poem

I let myself fall
into the language of night
totally intoxicated
by the quiet darkness
experienced and acquired
the bed belongs to daydreamers
stay awake bleary-eyed
the night says with certainty
as long as the day begins
    in the night

Revolution

permanent changes are declared
in our relationship
each day giving a fresh start
to the revolution
so as not to freeze to the routine
environment checking the strength
of dependence and
refreshing my feelings for you
I'd rather risk a split skull
like Trotsky suffering
for his theories

am I acting like Caesar
conquering new provinces for the empire
putting the world at risk

37

konstellationen

der amerikanische präsident
reiste zu gesprächen nach israel
anna-berta weilt derzeit in new york
während birgit sich in wien befindet
der österreichische bundeskanzler
in begleitung des vizekanzlers und
des bundespräsidenten losziehen
zum antrittsbesuch des neuen papstes
fahre ich mit clara nach bologna
dann mit doris nach venedig und rom
wie nun die deutsche bundeskanzlerin
mit vertretern der rüstungsindustrie
nach china und saudi-arabien
aufbricht zieht es den wirtschaftsminister
nach griechenland im gefolge einer
gruppe solaranlagenhersteller
keine beachtung in den medien
findet claudias reise nach budapest
gerd fliegt zum vögeln nach georgien

Constellations

the American President
travels for talks to Israel
Anna-Berta currently dwells in New York
while Birgit stays in Vienna
the Austrian Chancellor
accompanied by the Vice-Chancellor and
the Federal President set out
to visit the new Pope
I go with Clara to Bologna
and then with Doris to Venice and Rome
while the German Federal Chancellor
and a few arms industrialists make a trip
to China and Saudi Arabia
the Minister of Economics is heading
to Greece accompanied
by a batch of solar plant manufacturers
while Claudia travels to Budapest
no media coverage whatsoever for her
and for Gerd who flies for sex to Georgia

Stunde Null: Loop

Die Linde hat all ihre Blätter verloren
und vom Sommer blieb nichts als
der Wunsch dem alten Deutschland
noch einmal den Kopf zu kraulen
und zu versprechen dass seine Enkel
sich besser erinnern werden - was nützt
ein Gedicht wo die anwachsenden
Berge der Dinge zum Jodeln zwingen

Daniela Danz (GERMANY)

Daniela Danz was born in Eisenach in 1976. Her first poetry collection, entitled *Serimunt,* came out in 2004; it offered critical observations of everyday life in the East German countryside. Her next collection, *Pontus* (2009), examined the history and myths of the countries around the Black Sea. Her latest collection, *V,* was published in 2014. Her poems have been translated into several European languages.

Zero Hour: Loop

The lime tree had lost all its leaves
and nothing remained of the summer but
the desire to pet
old Germany's head again
and to promise that her grandchildren
would have better memories – what's the use
of a poem when the growing heaps of things
force you to yodel

Passage

Spätabends sind deine Schritte
noch im hellen Hof
worüber man spricht
hinter den Fenstern
das weißt du nicht

Je dunkler es wird je schwerer
die Luft die aus dem
Hauseingang fällt
wie die gezählten Stufen
riechen je und je anders
das wußtest du einmal

Was du weißt ist wenig vieles ist
alt geworden manches
ungültig ob die Robinien
im Mai blühen oder im
Juni hat einige Gründe
sie sind dir alle bekannt

Also setzt du dich auf die
Schwelle so still daß
das Licht ausgeht
wenn einer fragen würde
würdest du es erklären

Passage

Late at night your steps
are quiet in the bright yard
you don't know
what people are talking about
behind the windows

The darker it is the heavier
the air that gushes out
of the front door
from the steps counted so often
their smell is always different
from the familiar

What you know is not a lot
things become obsolete
or invalid   Whether the locust tree
blooms in May or in June
depends on several factors
you are aware of

So you sit on the
threshold so quietly that
the lights go out
if someone were to ask
you'd explain

Thin red line

der Säulenschatten zählt bis neun
und nichts ist übrig
daß dir eine Linie zieht
von hier bis in die Gischt
dein ganzes Wünschen reicht nicht hin
für ein Bunker unterm Berg
und in den Kammern Waffen
was du schaffst ist nur ein Arsenal
von viel zu leichten Tagen
das du zu Felde führen willst
wenn auf den Hügeln eine schmale
rote Linie vorrückt
denn du weißt: erst am Abend
ist es leicht
das Aufgesparte zu verzehren

Telepylos

Kein leichtes Boot im dunklen
Tunnelwasser kein Plätschern
eintauchender Ruder nur eine eiserne
Ration Homer: *im herrlichen Hafen*
die stählernen Buckel der Uboote
da könnte ein Mann ohne Schlaf
sich doppelten Lohn verdienen
nachts in Netzen die glänzenden
Rücken der Meeräschen tags
die Uboote mit Waffen beladend

Thin Red Line

the shadow of the pillar points to nine
and there is nothing left
that can draw a line for you
from here to the sea foam
all your wishes are not enough
for a bunker under the mountain
and weapons in the chambers
what you obtain is just an arsenal
of lightweight days
that you want to lead into battle
when a thin red line descends
onto the hills
because you know: only in the evening
is it easy
to consume what you've saved

Telepylos

No light boat in the dark
tunnel water no splashes
of dipping oars only Homer's
iron ration: in the marvellous port
the steel humps of submarines
there a man who never sleeps
could double his salary
catching silverside fish with a net
at night and loading the submarines
with weapons during the day

Durchschwimm die Bucht verbinde
ihre Ufer in einer Naht
aus Atemzug und Tauchen
solange an den Klippen das Meer
sich müht aus Kieseln Würfel
für ein Spielchen uns zu schleifen

Die Kamera im Dienst der Ethnologie

ich sah ein Foto auf dem ein Mann vom
Stamm der Schubi lachend seinen Körper
zeigt die Arme unterhalb der Achseln
eingeschnürt von breiten Reifen blieben

dünn wie die des Jungen der er war
darunter quollen strahlend die Muskeln
hervor des Mannes der er wurde

ich sah der Mensch ist ein Baum
der über seine Wunden fortwächst
das Fleisch die Rinde die eigene
Gestalt unser ganzer nutzloser Stolz

swimming across the bay
to connect its banks
with a seam of breathing and diving
while the sea strives
to polish pebbles on the cliffs
to play a little dice game with us

The Camera in the Service of Ethnology

I saw a photo of a man from
the tribe of Shubi showing off his body
and laughing his arms squeezed by
massive bracelets

were thin below the shoulders like those
of the boy he once was under the shiny
well-rounded muscles of the man he's become

I saw man as a tree
that keeps growing over its wounds
the flesh the bark our
shape all our useless pride

Deutsche Gedichte

Es steht nichts mehr zwischen den Zeilen
kein Platz zwischen den Zeilen
das Papier vollgeschrieben
mit dem Nichts von Heute.
Immer zu wenig
Blut in den Adern, immer
zu kalt.
Immer noch dasselbe hohle Getön
Kunststückchen darüber wie man
die Hände bewegt ohne zu arbeiten
und schicksalsschwer die Seele runzelt, um den Schatten
zu betören

Ludwig Fels (GERMANY / AUSTRIA)

Ludwig Fels was born in 1946 in Treuchtlingen, Franconia, and has been living in Vienna since 1983. In the 1960s, he was a factory worker and about the same time started writing. He's been a full-time writer since 1973. Apart from a few novels and plays, he has published nine poetry collections, the latest being *Wherever the End of the World Is* (2010). He was the recipient of the Hans Fallada Prize (1983) and the Wolfgang Köppen Prize (2004).

German Poems

There's nothing between the lines any more,
no space between the lines;
the sheet of paper is fully covered
with the nothingness of today.
There's always a deficit of
blood in the veins; it's ever
so cold.
Always the same hollow noise,
a little trick of making your hand move
without actually doing anything,
and making your soul look sullen to beguile
the shadows.

sag ich mal einfach so ist ja auch egal.
Vom Rand der Dinge kommen noch manchmal
Stimmen. Dort wird noch gekämpft
und verloren, dort gibt es noch diese
Leidenschaft der Besiegten und dieses
Lächeln über die Lügen der Liebe.

Nähe

Der Regen kommt jetzt jeden Abend
sagt sie
Wind geht am Strand
sagt sie
kalt, kein Mensch mehr hier
sagt sie
und ich sage du.
Ich bin allein
sagt sie
und ich, sage ich, bin ohne dich
und sie lacht und raucht
hör den Wind dahinter.
Der Regen kommt jetzt jeden Abend
sagt sie
nachts wird es kalt
sagt sie
ich sage, ich friere im Traum.

I say it plainly, as it doesn't matter.
From the edge of things sometimes come
voices. There's still fighting going on there,
battles being lost; there you can still find
the passion of the defeated and smiles
about the deceptiveness of love.

Nearness

These days it rains every evening
she says
The wind combs the beach
she says
it's chilly, people no longer come here
she says
and I say You.
I'm on my own
she says
and I say, I don't have you
and she laughs and smokes
hears the wind behind us.
These days it rains every evening
she says
nights grow cold
she says
I say, I'm freezing in this dream.

Ach, wirklich

Ach, wirklich, ich hab ein paar
Buecher geschrieben, kaum
Reisen gemacht, war
immer da
einfach immer da
wo nichts war
nie etwas sein wird
alles nicht der Rede wert.
Ach, wirklich, Gedichte, zum Heulen
komisch, wenn das Gewicht der Welt
herunterfaellt.

Liebe, achja

Ein Gedicht über die Liebe schreiben
vom Schlaf träumen, bevor man stirbt
ein Gedicht über die Liebe, aber
welches Gedicht über welche Liebe
und was, wenn die Liebe
gar keine Liebe war und das Leben
viel zu kurz für den ersten
Kuß?

Oh Yes Indeed

Oh yes indeed I've written
a couple of books, hardly
travelled at all, always
stayed here,
simply was here
where there's nothing
and nothing will ever be,
nothing worth mentioning.
Oh yes indeed, poetry, such a funny thing
it brings tears when the weight of the world
comes crashing down.

Love, oh Yeah

To write a poem about love,
to dream about sleeping, before you die
a poem about love – but
what kind of poem and about which love?
And what if that love
wasn't love at all and life
was far too short for the first
kiss?

Hospital

Der Geruch, der Geruch, er
schlägt sich nieder
auf den Mauern drinnen und draußen
Zeichen und Male, verfließende Schichten
jeder Ziegel, jede Scheibe
wie aus Schmerz gepreßt. Und:
die Pavillons haben grüne
Dächer aus Stacheldraht und Gras
und hier kann niemand sein
der Drogen nahm und Liebes-
lieder sang. Paar verzerrte
Riffs einer elektrischen
Gitarre weht es durch den Park
mit dem roten Rasen.
Und Jesus, er kommt
in den OP, sagt:
Keine Narkose!

Hospital

That smell, that smell, it's
sedimented on the walls
inside and out.
Signs and markings, overlapping
layers of paint; each brick,
each washer formed from pain. And
the pavilions have green
roofs made of grass and barbed wire,
and no drug-takers or
singers of love songs are
allowed here. A couple of distorted
electric guitar riffs are blown
through the park
along with red dust.
And Jesus, he comes
into the surgery and says:
No anaesthetic!

Gastspiel

Dieses ungenannte Land ist beschaffen
wie jedes andere. Beschriftet mit dem

Abstand zur Sonne. Die Parkwächterinnen
bewachen die Parks oder üben Verliebtsein.

Im Freilicht der Tage sind Hitze und Kälte
abwechselnd zu Gast mit ihrem Ensemble.

Nach der Arbeit feiern die Parkwächterinnen
Geburtstag. Die Kerzen flackern. Von Zeit

zu Zeit fallen Insekten, die frei sind in der
Wahl der Ziele, auf den Glanz ihrer Rücken.

Brigitte Fuchs (SWITZERLAND)

Brigitte Fuchs was born in Widnau, Switzerland, in 1951. She worked as a primary school teacher in Rorschach and in the cantons of St. Gallen and Aargau, and later as a literary editor. Since 1986 she has published eight collections of her poems, the latest being *And the Stones Danced* (2014), as well as children's books. She lives in Teufent.

Guest Performance

This unnamed country is designed
like any other. Labelled with

the distance from the Sun. The park keepers
guard the parks or make love.

Out in the open, hot and cold days alternate
their visits, presenting an ensemble.

After work the park keepers celebrate
their birthdays. The candles flicker. From time

to time insects, free to choose
their targets, fall onto their glossy backs.

Leoparden

Leoparden treten aus der Schwärze
jäh heraus auf diese Bühnenlichtung
sanfte Nacken scharfer Blick

Da stehe ich mir fehlt das Wort für
guten Morgen

Wie kommen diese ausgedachten
Schönen überhaupt hierher in meine
wildtierarme Gegend

Lustlos fliegt der Engel weg –
ich weiss nicht spielt das für mich zur

Zeit noch irgend eine Rolle

Himmel. Nochmal.

Schön. Er weiss also mehr als ich.
Sein Auge wacht über jeden Griff
zu den Sternen. Über das Paradies
des Erdenklichen. Über Verkleidung
und Masken. Ich kenne das Spiel.
Die Dramaturgie. Trotzig trete ich
in seine nicht nachweisbaren Spuren.
Lege Gedichte aus: Leimruten. Schlingen.
Des Teufels laute Schwester schaut
vorbei. Singt die Schlange in den Schlaf.

Leopards

Leopards all of a sudden come out
of the blackness and onto this stage
gentle neck sharp look

Here I stand unable to find the word
for good morning

How did it come about
that these invented beauties are here in our
not-so-rich-in-wildlife zone

An angel flies away, indifferent –
I do not know if this

matters much to me just now

Heaven. Revisited.

Nice. So he knows more than I do.
His eyes watch over every lever
for the stars. Over the paradise
of the conceivable. Over garments
and masks. I know this game.
The plot. Reluctantly I follow
in his invisible steps.
Press poems from: limes. Slings.
The devil's loud sister looks
away. Sings the snake to sleep.

Zitate

Alle Flüsse fliessen ins Meer das Meer
wird nicht voll. Auch die Frau. Und die
Sonne. Atemlos jagen sie zurück an den
Ort. Trachten von neuem danach Frau
und Sonne zu sein. Behalte den Flug im
Gedächtnis schreibt die Dichterin der Vogel
ist sterblich. Und die Frau dreht sich. Dreht
sich um sich. Um den Fluss um das Meer
um den Ort und den Mann. Dazwischen.

*Anmerkung der Autorin: Der Text wurde angeregt durch ein Zitat der
persischen Dichterin Forugh Farochzad.*

Hangar

Ein Lob auf diesen trockenen Standort
Kein Rost setzt an auf den Eisenflügeln
der Schwalben

Die Finger bewegen sich flugs
Sie knöpfen Hemden auf sie schlendern
über die Boulevards der Körper
Stecken Wörter in Brand

Am Ende des Sommers ziehen sie
die mechanischen Vögel auf
und werfen sie gegen die Wand
der Wolken

Quotations

All the streams flow into the sea; the sea
never overfills. Same with the woman. With
the sun. Breathless, they rush back to
the familiar place. Striving to be the woman
and the sun again. Bear the flight
in mind writes the poetess the bird
is mortal. And the woman turns. Turns
around herself. Around the river around the sea
around the place around the man. In between them.

*Author's note: The poem was inspired by a quotation from the Persian poet
Forugh Farokhzad.*

Hangar

Praise for this dry shelter
No rust settles on the swallows'
iron wings

The fingers move hastily
around a shirt button as they stroll
along the boulevards of the body
Set words on fire

At the end of summer they pull out
these mechanical birds
and throw themselves against the wall
of clouds

Verzagt

Im Schließfach eines Fernbahnhofs in B.
Fand sich die Leiche eines neugebornen Kindes,
Kaum eine Woche alt. Die Nabelwunde war noch frisch.

Noch war der Name auf der Haut nicht angetrocknet,
Kaum sichtbar das Geschlecht, da lag das Bündel
Schon festverschnürt zur Reise

In einen andern Automaten-Limbo, in ein andres Licht.

Durs Grünbein (GERMANY)

Durs Grünbein was born in Dresden in 1962, and studied theatre at Humboldt University in Berlin. In 2005, he held the position of Max Kade Distinguished Visiting Professor at Dartmouth College. Since 2006, Grünbein has been a visiting professor at the Academy of Fine Arts in Düsseldorf, and has also lived in Rome. He has published twelve collections of his poems, the latest being *Colossus in the Fog* (2012), and a number of books of essays, not only on literary topics but also on quantum physics, neurology and philosophy. In 2006, he was awarded the Berlin Prize for Literature; in 2012, the Thomas Tranströmer Award (Sweden).

Despondent

In the locker of a railway station in B.
the body of a new-born child was found,
barely a week old. The umbilical wound still fresh.

Even the name written on the skin hadn't yet dried.
Shortly after the gender was determined, the body was already
firmly bundled up for a journey

into another machine limbo, into another light.

Belebter Bach

mit alten Autoreifen, Glas,
Sperrmüll und der Attrappe
eines kleinen Wehrs

aus Zellophan und Schrott,
in dem inmitten Schaums
auf einem Ölfilm ausgesetzt

ein grüner Badefisch sich
zwischen Zweigen schaukelnd
leicht um seine Achse dreht.

Kommt
Wellen klaren Wassers, kommt.

Der Cartesische Hund

Wedelnd um jedes Nein das ihn fortschleift
Worte wie Flöhe im Fell, die Schnauze im Dreck

Ohren angelegt auf der Flucht vor den Nullen
Gejagt von den kleineren Übeln ins Allergrößte

Müde der leeren Himmel, die Kehle blank
Gehorcht er dem Ersten das kommt und ihn denkt

Busy Brook

accommodates old car tyres, glass,
bulky refuse and a makeshift
little weir

consisting of cellophane and scrap metal
a green fish bathes itself
in the froth

stuck to the oily film
it dodges branches
rotates freely around its axis

Come
waves of clear water, come

The Cartesian Dog

Wagging around each negation that drags him away
Words resemble fleas in the fur, the snout in the dirt

Ears dropped in flight from the zeros
Chased away from smaller troubles toward the biggest one

Tired of the empty sky; his throat exposed
He follows the first person who comes and gives him a thought

In der Provinz 4
(CAMPANIA)

Wie der Gekreuzigte lag dieser Frosch
Plattgewalzt auf dem heißen Asphalt
Der Landstraße. Offenen Mauls,

Bog sich zum Himmel, von Sonne gedörrt,
Was von fern einer Schuhsohle glich –
Ein Amphibium aus älterer Erdzeit,
Unter die Räder gekommen im Sprung.

Keine Auferstehung als in den Larven
Der Fliegen, die morgen schlüpfen werden.

Durch welche Öffnung entweicht der Traum?

Fisch im Medium

Was gemeint ist heißt Name, was verschwiegen bleibt Ding.
Weitverzweigt sind die Sätze zu jeder Schandtat bereit.
Peinliche Immanenz... In die Gödelschen Öden verrannt
Wird das Geschwätz wie der heilige Geldumlauf paranoid.
Der tägliche Aktienindex, ein Coup, gibt dem Spiel
Das Maß aller Dinge, die Regeln für Schicksal im Text.
Die Spiegel, ins Kühlfach gelegt, werden blind. Feierlich
Schwelt in Archiven und Banken das humanistische Gold.
»Ich hätte mich gern wie ein Fisch in den Medien bewegt.«

In the Province 4
(CAMPANIA)

This frog was, like the Crucified One,
flattened on the hot tarmac
of a motorway. Open-mouthed,

twisted toward the sky, parched by the sun …
From a distance it resembled a shoe sole,
an amphibian from a remote geological epoch
whose leap ended under the wheels.

No resurrection here, only
flies will emerge from the larvae tomorrow.

Through which opening does a dream escape?

Fish in Medium

What's meant has a name, what's hushed up remains a thing.
Branching sentences are ready for mischief.
Embarrassing immanence … On the wrong track of Gödel's
    boredom
Chatter becomes paranoid like the circulation of holy money.
The daily stock index, a coup that makes a game
The measure of all things, the rules for putting fate into a text.
Mirrors, placed in the freezer, go blind. The gold of humanism
Decays solemnly in archives and banks.
"I'd love to move like fish in the media."

yoshiyuki park

warme erleuchtung in der nacht
ins gras gerammte riemchenschuhe
um das vierbeinige kopflose fabelwesen
zu stabilisieren im erdreich denn
diese nacht verschluckt das überflüssige

dies ist erkundung auf engstem raum
nach fingern im grashaufen: unzählbar
den weg nur beleuchtet durch das
seidenschimmern eines kleides
keinerlei straßenlaternen mehr hier

Annette Hagemann (GERMANY)

Annette Hagemann was born in Münster, Westphalia, in 1967. She studied German literature and anthropology at Göttingen University, and later worked as a freelance journalist and as a museum educator in the Lower Saxony State Museum, Hanover. Since 2001 she has been working in the Literature House, Hanover. In 2009, she published her first collection of poetry, entitled *Competing with the Sun God* (Wehrhahn Publishing). Also in 2009, she received the literary scholarship of Lower Saxony. Her second poetry collection, *Siren of the Shower Room*, was published by Horlemann Publishing, Berlin, in 2014.

Yoshiyuki Park

warm enlightenment in the night
sandal heels driven into the soil
to steady the four-legged headless
mythical creature because this night
swallows what's superfluous

fingers explore the confined spaces
in the grass heap: uncountable
paths illuminated only by the
silky shimmer of a dress
no more street lamps here

china town

fast hätte ich den glücksdrachen gekauft
an dem morgen auf dem chinesischen markt
da bauten sie noch die stände auf und schon
hatte ich ihn gesehen: sehr freundlich
sehr entgegenkommend im wind
mit einem großen grinsenden kopf aus papier
oder pappmaché gelockten augenbrauen:
einem kopf aus lachsfarbenem papier
und einem lachsfarbenen schweif
der zwei bis drei meter lang im wind schlug
bereit zum ausritt das konnte man sehen
wir lachten uns an und beinahe hätte ich
ihn mitgenommen: egal zu welchem preis
doch ich war noch nicht soweit für so viel glück

telefonzelle (new york 1988)

puerto rico das war schön
die alte heimatliche hitze
holt man sich hier im norden
eben durch den körper der mutter
da steht sie mit schwarz ondulierten locken
ein blau und beige geblümtes kleid und die figur
einer vase: schmal am kopf und an den fesseln
dazwischen viel leib für blumenwasser und für rum
puertoricanische kochkünste ungeborene kinder

Chinatown

I almost bought a lucky dragon
at the Chinese market this morning
they had just started putting up the stands
when I noticed it: very friendly
very deferential with the wind
with a big grinning head made from paper
or papier-mâché and curly eyebrows: a head
made from pink salmon-coloured paper
and a pink salmon-coloured tail
two to three metres long trembling in the wind
ready to ride as far as my eyes could see
we gave each other a smile and I almost
snapped it up no matter what it cost
but I wasn't quite ready for so much luck

Phone Booth (New York, 1988)

After Helen Levitt's photograph of the same name

Puerto Rico that was nice
the old homelike heat
here in the north you just get it
through the body of the mother
who stands with her black coiffured curls
a blue and beige floral dress and the shape
of a vase: narrow at the top and at the ankles,
in between much room for flower water and rum,
Puerto Rican cooking skills, unborn children

und von außen an sie angelehnt mehrere
geborene in verschiedenen (kleinen) größen
wovon keines den clan verlässt: nicht mal
wenn sie die telefonzelle betritt

pension in blankenese

morgens woanders erwachen
nach einer ruhigen nacht
vorm fenster ein abhang voller bäume
unzählige blätter in bewegung
ein ewiges rauschen: diese blätter
und bäume sehen genauso aus
wie zu caspar david friedrichs zeit
es ist genau die gleiche schönheit
zu der wir immer zurückkehren können
ich dehne und rolle mich auf die seite
dann richte ich mich auf um die ersten
dinge des tages zu tun
zum beispiel an dich zu denken
ich kann für mich sein
und ich kann für dich sein
und manchmal beides zugleich

and from the outside leaning against her
several little ones in various (small) sizes
none of them leaving the clan: not even
when she enters the phone booth

B&B in Blankenese

in the morning waking up someplace else
after a peaceful night
out the window a hillside with trees
multitudes of leaves in motion
an eternal murmur: these leaves
and trees look just like they did
in Caspar David Friedrichs' time
it is exactly the kind of beauty
we can always return to
I stretch and roll onto my side
then I get up to do
the first things of the day
such as thinking of you
I can live by myself
or I can live for you
and sometimes both at once

bienengeflüster

als wandbild steh ich
hinter allen frauen
die nach mir kamen
als unsichtbare ikone
begleite ich dich
mild und fleißig zerreiße ich die
weißen nähte deiner träume
nacht um nacht
insektenaugen habe ich
wirst du einmal wieder tief
mit deinem blick in sie hineingeraten
ich stehe als statue
an deiner schwelle und summe
jeden an und jede die zu dir will
ich summe ich steche
mein stern meine wabe und sage:
dieser bann endet nicht

Whispering Bees

as a mural I stand
behind all women
who came later than I
an invisible icon
I follow you
gentle and diligent I tear
the white seams of your dreams
night after night
my insect eyes
will you some day plunge
deep into them again
I stand as a statue
at your threshold and buzz
at everyone who wants to
come near you
I buzz I sting
my star my honeycomb and I say:
this spell will not end

Erwachen

Eine schöne Amsel öffnet mir morgens
die Augen. Sie singt im Zypressengrün
das Lied der Liebe von einst
Eine schöne Amsel löscht mir am Morgen
die Träume. Ich sitze mitten
im Licht ich bin wirklich da.

Ulla Hahn (GERMANY)

Ulla Hahn was born in 1946 in Sauerland. She studied German language and literature, sociology and history at the University of Cologne. She later worked as a lecturer at the same university, and as a literary editor for Radio Bremen. In 1981 she published her first book of poems, *Heart over Head.* All in all, she has published three novels and eleven collections of poems, the latest being *Further Words (2011)*. A volume of her *Collected Poems* was published in 2013 in Munich by Deutsche Verlag-Anstalt. In 2002, she was awarded the German Book Prize; in 2010, the Ida Dehmel Prize. She lives in Hamburg.

Awakening

A charming blackbird makes me open my eyes
in the morning. In the cypress grove it sings
of love and of the days of yore.
A charming blackbird erases my morning
dreams. I am sitting in the middle of it,
in full light. I am really here.

Ich bin die Frau

Ich bin die Frau
die man wieder mal anrufen könnte
wenn das Fernsehen langweilt

Ich bin die Frau
die man wieder mal einladen könnte
wenn jemand abgesagt hat

Ich bin die Frau
die man besser nicht einlädt
zur Hochzeit

Ich bin die Frau
die man lieber nicht fragt
nach einem Foto vom Kind

Ich bin die Frau
die keine Frau ist
fürs Leben.

Blinde Flecken

Daß wir so uneins sind hält uns zusammen
du dort ich hier – wir sind auf andrer Fahrt:
Dein Istgewesen mein Eswirdnochkommen
zwei blinde Flecken in der Gegenwart
die uns gehört wie Träume vorm Erwachen
wenn wir schon wissen daß wir Träumer sind
die mit uns spielt ein Weilchen in den Winden
bis jedes hier und dort sich wiederfindet.

I am the Woman

I am the woman
you might ring again
when you're bored of television

I am the woman
you could invite again
if someone else cancelled

I am the woman
you wouldn't invite
to a wedding

I am the woman
you wouldn't ask
for a photo of her child

I am the woman
who isn't somebody's woman
for life.

Blind Spots

We're so divided that it keeps us together.
You're there, I'm here – we are taking different journeys:
you're bound for Has-Been, I for Will-Happen.
Two blind spots in the present
that belongs to us – like dreams before awakening
if we already know that we are dreamers –
and plays games in the wind with us for a short while
until everything around falls into place.

Nach Jahr und Tag

Ein Waggon fährt vorbei
Er hat Kohle geladen

Männer links Frauen rechts
Zu den Kabinen im Freibad

Schuhe liegen auf einem Haufen
Im Sommerschlußverkauf

Haare werden geschnitten
Zu einer neuen Frisur

Menschen gehen ins Bad
Zum Baden

Ein Feuer brennt
Es wärmt

Rauch steigt auf
Eine Kerze verlischt

After So Many Years

A railway carriage passes by
It's loaded with coal

Men to the left women to the right
Into the changing rooms by the outdoor pool

Shoes lying in a pile
It's the end-of-summer sale

Hair being cut
A new hairstyle

People go to the pool
To swim

A fire's burning
It warms

Smoke rises
A candle extinguished

Keine Tochter

Ja der Kuchen ist gut – Ich habe
nie gern Süßes gegessen – Ich esse
gern noch ein Stück

Nein mir geht es nicht schlecht.
Viel Arbeit Ja. Älter werde ich auch.
Noch kein Mann? Nein kann Mann.

Vorm Eigenheim mit Frau und Kind
des Sohnes wuchs der Ableger
von der Clematis vorm Elternhaus an.

Überm Fernsehen schläfst du ein.
Dein Kopf sackt nach vorn deine Schulter
auf meine. Ich halte still.

Näher kommst du mir nicht.
Ich bin dir wie vor meiner Zeugung
so fern. Verzeih ich möchte
auch keine Tochter haben wie mich.

No Daughter

Yes, the cake is good – I've
never liked eating sweets – I'll
take one more slice.

No, I am not too bad.
Pretty busy. Yes. Getting older, too.
Haven't got a husband yet? No, I haven't.

In front of the house where your son's wife
and child live grows the off-shoot of
the clematis from your parents' house.

While watching TV you fall asleep.
Your head tilts forward, your shoulder
next to mine. I don't move.

You come no closer.
I am as far from you as I was before
I was conceived. Forgive me but I wouldn't want
to have a daughter like me either.

[Unter unzähligen Gründen]

Unter unzähligen Gründen ist der beste
der letzte. Und gäbe es andre bewohnbare Welten
so bliebe doch alles beim alten. Denn
jede mögliche Welt ist die einzig reale. Ist die Wirklichkeit
in der man grade lebt. Strebt
aber alles nach Vielzahl und Buntheit gibt's wenig
zu wundern. Wird das Unmögliche
bald zum Normalsten. Alles – so muss man
wohl sagen – ist nie genug. Schon gar nicht ein einziges
Leben. Wie dieses zum Beispiel.

Felix Philipp Ingold (SWITZERLAND)

Felix Philipp Ingold was born in 1942 in Basel. He studied history and philosophy at the University of Basel and at the Sorbonne in Paris. He worked as a journalist and as a radio presenter, and is now Professor Emeritus at the University of St. Gallen. He has been published as a poet, a novelist, an essayist and a literary translator. His recent collections are *Word Acquisition: Early Poems* (Basel 2005), *The Russian Way: Poems* (Munich 2007), and *Shape of the Day: Poems about Time* (Graz / Vienna, 2007). He has also translated many classical and contemporary Russian poets into German. He lives in Zurich.

[Among countless reasons]

Among countless reasons the best
is the last. Were there other habitable worlds
everything there would still be the same – because
each possible world is the only real one. It's the reality
in which we live. Still, all things search
for diversity and colour; it's
no wonder. The impossible will soon
become normal. Everything, one can be
bound to say, is not enough. Least of all
somebody's life. This one, for instance.

Tierleben 0

Im Anfang war
das Wort ein Ort. Noch
fern vom Namen
und noch ungeschieden
vom Ruch – Geist
wie Bewegung! – der Natur.
Ruht nah
dem Rätsel das die Lösung
ist. Das Knirschen
dieses oder jenes Kontinents.
Das Wummern der Meere.
Das Pochen wo
das Blut beginnt. Wo der
Ja! - Leib klart. Und
wie im Märch...
Das Spieglein an der Wand.
Wie's tobt. Die Schönheit im Auge
des Andern.

Nahst

Wo
ist die Nacht.
Dort
deine Hand mein heiserstes
Organ. Laut
aufgedreht die Lust.

From "Animal Life"

In the beginning was
the word for place. Farther
from the name
and still indistinguishable
from the stench – spirit
as movement! – of nature.
Close to the puzzle,
which is
a solution. The grinding
of a continent, one or other.
The rumbling of the sea.
The throbbing where
the blood comes from. Where
the Yes!-body appears. And,
like in a fairy-tale …
The mirror on the wall.
And rage. Beauty in the eye
of a bystander.

Drawing Near

Where
is the night?
There,
your hand and my husky
member. Lust
grows intense.

Wo
ist die Naht.
Uns trennt
ein Glück. Das knirschende
Ende wovon.

Ausgesungen

* * *

Dieselbe Rose
macht den Mittag aus. Schön
dunkelt's. Zu
löschen ich auch.

* * *

Licht is die agonie
der Nacht. Nie
tagt es nicht. Wir sind
immer zu lesen.

Where
is the seam?
Happiness
separates us. It all ends with
a grinding sound.

From "Aftersong"

* * *

This rose
quenches the noon. Beautiful
twilight. I too
will vanish.

* * *

Light is the agony
of night. No day
without dawn. One
can always read us.

[Hören auf das was nie]

Hören auf das was nie
spricht. Achtsam
liegt sich's schwerer. Wer
da wacht am einen Pol
der Lust. Kein
Suhlen nicht. Licht ist
das Ziel. Da. Es
harrt.
........Was löscht die Mittagswut. ...
..... die Sille ist was sich gehört.

[Listen to what never]

Listen to what never
speaks. The attentive
land harder. Who
keeps watch at the pole
of pleasure. No one's
floundering. Light is
the target. Here.
It's in waiting.
.... What cancels the noon rage. ...
.... the future is what belongs here.

Fahrt in die Endlichkeit

Im Garten von Monk's house die Asche
unter den gestürzten Ulmen, die Asche

von Virginia Woolf, die nutzte die downs
als mintgrüne Ausflucht und darin den kalten

River Ouse. Über die hölzerne Brücke bei Southease,
in deren Pfeilern sich die Leiche verfing,

fuhren wir, spielten auf dem Xylophon
ein Wehmutslied, ein Requiem auf Rappelbalken.

Mathias Jeschke (GERMANY)

Mathias Jeschke was born in Lüneburg in 1963. He studied Theology at Göttingen, Heidelberg and Rostock universities. He is a full-time writer and an occasional book editor, and has published three collections of his poems, *Windland* (1999), *The Great Blue Heron* (2006) and *Boat and the Beast* (2007), as well as academic and children's books. He lives in Stuttgart.

Journey in the Finitude

In the garden of Monk's House, the ashes
under the fallen elms, the ashes

of Virginia Woolf, who used the Downs
as a mint green escape, same as the cold

River Ouse. Along the wooden bridge at Southease,
where the corpse got caught among the posts,

we drove, playing a melancholy song
on the xylophone, rattling timber's requiem.

Fahrt im Sommer

Zum Fluß hinunter
die Biegung der Straße. Vom Rücksitz
die Tochter rief: Meer!

Von der Brücke aus
das Ruderboot im Gegenlicht, Vierer
ohne Steuermann.

Der Körper hob sich
übers Wasser auf vier Beinen, leicht,
ein Wasserläufer.

Auf den Seen
der Kindheit, dem Asphalt die Fahrt
hinaus ins Gleißen.

Die Sonne ohne Falsch
und Schwäche wie eines Ruderers
Händedruck.

Summer Trip

Down to the river,
the curvature of the road. From the back seat,
my daughter's scream: *The sea!*

From the bridge,
the rowing boat in backlight, four
without steersman.

The body overhung
across the water on four legs, light,
a water strider.

On the lakes
of childhood, the ride on asphalt
out into the glare.

The sun without a fault
and weakness resembling
an oarsman's handshake.

Kleines Geläut

Erneut das Licht der Welt erblickt
am sandigen Rand.

Muscheln, Buch und Stein
zum Eigentum und diese leise Stimme.

Scherenschnitte, die Porträts
der schwarzen Kühe vor dem Himmel.

Auch das rostige Lied des Fasans,
der Wind, der in den Bäumen blättert.

Und in den Wellen dieses Ding,
das singt, das unverrückte Herz.

Unterwegs

Der Nachbar in der Hängematte
auf einem Meer aus Ruhe.

Das leere Logbuchblatt des Himmels,
er notiert den Ort:

Du hörst das Füllfederschaben
seines Schnarchens.

Auf stillen Wellen des Mittags
fährt er hinüber.

Small Bells

Once again a new light flickers
on the sandy edge.

Shells, a book and a stone
for the property, this quiet voice.

Silhouettes, portraits
of the black cows against the sky.

Also the raucous song of the pheasant,
the wind that leafs through the trees.

And in the waves that thing
which sings, the sane heart.

On the Way

The neighbour in the hammock
above a sea of tranquillity.

The empty logbook of the sky,
he marks his location:

you hear the feather-scrapes
of his snoring.

On the quiet waves of the noon
he rows across.

Ohne Ruder. Das Boot ist er selbst.
Das Ufer in ihm.

Spiel zwischen Erde und Himmel

Im Augenwinkel der Sturz.
Schrill, scharf gellt der Pfiff.

Ich wende mich hin,
doch niemand gefoult am Boden.

Es war eine Schwalbe.
Ich stehe auf der Lichtung und öffne mich.

Die Vögel jubeln,
die Bäume schwenken ihr Fahnengrün.

Erneut ein schriller Pfiff.
Erwartung wächst.

Da trifft es mich:
Ich stehe am Punkt für den Freistoß.

Without oars. He himself is the boat.
The shore is in him.

Match between Earth and Heaven

In the corner of my eye, a tumble.
High-pitched, shrill sound of a whistle.

I turn back,
but no one lies on the ground having being fouled.

It was a dive.
I'm standing in the clearing, open on all sides.

The birds rejoice,
the trees wave their green flags.

Again, a shrill whistle.
Expectation grows.

Then it dawns on me: I'm on the spot
the free kick is to be taken from.

Vater und Sohn

Ein einziges Abstandhalten
und Beieinanderstehn
mit schlenkernden Armen.
Der Vater die Uniform,
der Sohn mit den Rastazöpfen.
Der Vater im Rucksack Preußen,
der Sohn auf dem Surfbrett
zur Mündung der Flüsse hinaus.
Der Vater auf Reisen,
der Sohn die innere Emigration.
Der Vater die Briefe,
der Sohn schweigt.

Uwe Kolbe (GERMANY)

Uwe Kolbe was born in 1957 in East Berlin. He published his first poems in 1976; soon after that he completed a course in literature at the Institute of Literature named for Johannes Becher. In 1980, after the publication of his first collection titled *Born into This,* he was banned from publishing anything in East Germany and put under surveillance. In 1986, he moved to West Germany and settled in Hamburg. He has since published ten collections of poems, including *Not Entirely Platonic (1994), Vineta (1998), Secret Celebrations (2008)* and *Songs of Lietzen* (2012), as well as a novel. He works as a free-lance writer in Berlin.

Father and Son

Being so far apart,
yet so close together,
with their arms down.
The father in a uniform,
the son with dreadlocks.
The father with Prussia in his shoulder bag,
the son on his surfboard
gliding toward the river mouth.
The father on a journey,
the son in inner emigration.
The father writing letters,
the son keeping schtum.

Vater, ders locker nimmt,
Sohn zu dem Herzen.
Einander Kampf ohne Regel,
ernster als auf dem Spieplatz je,
länger als lebenslang.
Nie sterben die Väter,
hört man, seit Ohren sind,
und selten leben die Söhne.

Sailor's All

Und wieder ein Liebesgedicht
vom Rande der Katastrophen
(war's terroristischer Mord?
war's Flut und war's Hunger
oder schlicht
Shareholder's Value?).
Wir hatten anderes gelernt
und anderes versprochen
in einem der vorigen Leben,
unter dem Segel Hoffnung
im Industriezeitalter,
im Atomzeitalter,
im Ismus im Ismus im Ismus.
Was bleibt aber,
ist ein Liebesgedicht,
kleines, beharrliches Lied,
fast nichts.

The father taking life easy,
the son taking it all to heart.
Their fight is a no-rule one,
a no-nonsense one;
it lasts longer than a lifetime.
Fathers never die,
we hear from time immemorial.
As for sons, they rarely live.

Sailor's All

Once again a love poem
from the brink of disaster
(a murder by a terrorist?
a flood and hunger
or just
a stock market crash?)
We learned other things,
and were promised other things
in one of our previous lives,
under the sail of Hope
in the industrial age,
in the nuclear age,
in the world of -ism -ism -ism.
What remains with us
is a love poem,
a catchy little song,
almost nothing at all.

Landpartie mit E. F.

Es ist banal,
sagen die Besitzer der Gärten.
Es ist für dich, sagen die Vögel.

Ist es im Internet?
fragen die Jüngsten.
Es ist das Netz, das mich hält, sage ich.

Ist das ein Gedicht?
mäkeln Gebildete.
Ich weiß, es ist ein schöner Augenblick.

Sie lacht,
die kleine Göttin
an meiner Seite

Hineingeboren

Hohes weites grünes Land,

zaundurchsetzte Ebene.
Roter
Sonnenbaum am Horizont.

Der Wind ist mein
und mein die Vögel.

Picnic with E. F.

It is banal,
the owners of the garden say.
It is for you, the birds say.

Is it on the Internet?
the youngster inquires.
It is the net that holds me, I say.

Is it a poem?
intellectuals grumble.
I know it's a beautiful moment.

She laughs,
the little goddess
by my side.

Born into That

High, wide and green land,

the wire-fenced plain.
Red
sunlit tree at the horizon.

The wind is mine
and so are birds.

Kleines grünes Land enges,
Stacheldrahtlandschaft.
Schwarzer
Baum neben mir.
Harter Wind.
Fremde Vögel.

Nirgendwo mehr hin

Werden auf der Brücke bleiben,
eines in des andern Armen,
küssen sich, weit offen Augen
werden in den Mond sehn.

Haben Vater, Mutter wohl,
haben sie vergessen.
Sind so jung und schon so schwer,
wenn sie sich im Kreis drehn.

Werden Himmeln und Laternen
Liebe und den Ausbruch schwören.
Doch die Lichter, Straßen bleiben
stumm, es wird nur Wind wehn.

Werden von der Brücke nicht mehr,
nicht für Eltern, für die Katz,
nur noch sich und sich gehören,
nirgendwo mehr hin gehn.

Small green land narrows;
barbed wire landscape.
Tree next to me
black.
Fierce wind.
Strange birds.

Nowhere to Go

They'll remain on the bridge,
embracing,
kissing, eyes wide open,
looking at the moon.

They probably have fathers, mothers;
they have forgotten. So young
and already with such a heavy burden,
it's hard to turn within the circle.

They take vows of love and pain
before the sky and the lanterns.
But the lights and the streets remain
silent; there is only wind.

No longer on the bridge
for their parents or for anyone else;
belonging only to themselves;
nowhere else to go.

Kleine Welt Runde mit F.

Alles, was ich brauche
Um mich: Du, will sagen
Bist der Halt, aber drehst dich
Mit mir im Kreis.
Wir beschreiben uns selbst
Im Drehen erst richtig:
Mann und Frau
Bis das Karussell still steht
Halten wir stand.

Anton G. Leitner (GERMANY)

Anton G. Leitner was born in Munich in 1961. He studied law and philosophy at Munich University. Since 1993 he has been working as a publisher, editor and critic. He has also edited a number of important anthologies of poetry and the notable poetry magazine, *Das Gedicht.* He published nine collections of poems (most of them with DTV/Hanser, Munich), the latest being *The Truth About Uncle Spam and Other Revealing Poems* (2011), as well as a book of essays. Between 1980 and 2013, he edited more than thirty anthologies for prominent German publishers, most of them of poetry. He lives in Wessling in Southern Bavaria.

A Short Round-the-World Trip with F.

Everything I need
Around me: you, I mean,
My foothold. But join me
In the revolving loop.
It is in rotation that we
Describe ourselves correctly:
A man and a woman.
Until the carousel comes to a halt,
We will stand firm.

Die Bojen flüstern

Noch sieht der
Mond schwarz.

Unruhig wälzt sich
das Salz.

In den Bergen
stiftet man
Brand.

Die Aussicht
brennt durch.

Der Morgen bricht mit
Wellen an den
Tag.

Buoys Whisper

The moon still looks
black.

The salt tosses around
restlessly.

Somebody starts a fire
on top of a hill.

The scenery
burns out.

The waves of the morning
crash
upon the day.

Zu verkaufen

Man beschließt Abreisen
in eine andere Zone.
– Karl Krolow

Auch das geschlossene
Fenster hält nicht

Dicht, die Küste
Fegt ein redseliger

Wind. Wir wechseln
Worte, z. B. über

Den Salzgehalt
Der Luft oder

Pasteten von Enten
Leber. Wer streichelt

Unser tägliches
Brot so sanft

Besingt das Radio
Die Liebe in allen

Lagen. Bitte zieh
Den Stecker und

Häng das Schild
Raus.

For Sale

They decide to depart
for another zone.
– Karl Krolow

Even the closed window
Doesn't shut

Tight enough. The coast
Swept by a muttering

Wind. We exchange
Words, like

Salinity
Air or

Duck liver pie.
Who caresses

Our daily bread
So gently

The radio sings of
Love in all

Circumstances. Please
Pull the plug and

Hang the sign
Outside.

Herr Endlich sprintet

Nach Büroschluß
Heim.

Ich nütze
Deinen Vorsprung

Für ein Hintertreffen
Mit mir

Nicht, sagt er
Noch so

Vor sich hin
Dann nichts mehr

Im Anzug
Ein Skelett

Trägt zwei
Lagen Wurst

Und Käse
Zwischen Akten

Rastet Vollkorn
Aus.

Mr. Finally

Rushes home
After office hours.

*I won't take
Advantage*

*Of you losing ground
To me,*

He says
Just this

And nothing
Else

A skeleton
In a suit

Carrying
Between the files

Two layers
Of sausages and cheese

Wholemeal
Freak-out

Ersthelfer

Klebt das Pflaster
Am Hirn oder

Das Hirn am
Pflaster?

Frag nur
Damit du

Was
Lernst und

Mach das
Hirn

Weg vom
Pflaster.

First Aid

Is the patch stuck
To the brain or

The brain to
The patch?

Ask away
So you can

Learn
Something

And keep the
Brain

Separate from
The patch.

Toilette eines Cafés

auf dem weissen Lavabo
ein schwarzer Spazierstock
als hätte jemand plötzlich
das Gehen verlernt

Sabine Naef (SWITZERLAND)

Sabine Naef was born in 1974 in Lucerne, Switzerland. She studied Germanic and Romance languages at Zurich University, and also in Lausanne and Bordeaux. She is regarded as a master of the poetic miniature. She has published three collections: *Time Dump* (1998), *For Days I Wanted to Turn the Corner* (2001) and *Slight Dizziness* (2005). She has also collaborated with visual artists and musicians, and recorded two CDs of jazz music subsequently released in Switzerland. After spending a few years in Berlin, she is now living in the city of her birth.

Café Bathroom

across the white basin
a black walking stick
as though somebody suddenly
abandoned the practice of walking

[auf die Straße gestellte Möbel]

auf die Straße gestellte Möbel
halb blinde Spiegel
winzige Tassen
die Briefträgerin verliert kein Wort
Kaktusstacheln an den Fingern

[auf leisen Sohlen]

auf leisen Sohlen
der Zeitlupenkellner
bedient die letzten Gäste
und gewinnt die Zuneigung
einer Tulpe
der Mond trägt eine Augenbinde
pausenlos

[furniture out on the street]

furniture out on the street
half-blind mirrors
tiny cups
the postwoman doesn't utter a word
cactus thorns on her fingers

[soft-footed waiter]

soft-footed waiter
slow to serve
the last guests
wins the affection
of a tulip
the moon wears a blindfold
all night long

[selbst beim Umblättern]

selbst beim Umblättern
der Buchseiten
zwinkert er uns zu
der Tod
schwarz-weiß
geschminkt
Postskriptum

Dämmerung

die Laternen strecken
unaufhaltsam ihre Fühler aus
ein Mann hält inne
den Hut in der Hand
eine Taube hält Zwiesprache
mit dem fliehenden Tag

[even while turning over]

even while turning over
pages of books
he winks at us
Death
black and white
makeup
postscript

Twilight

the lanterns relentlessly
stick out their feelers
a man pauses
hat in hand
a dove maintains a dialogue
with the receding day

Schädlich

immer dröhnt die
eisenbahn in meinem
kopf. alarm schlagen
die ampeln eins
vor elf. noch
einmal grün in
leeren straßen. geh
ich nicht los.

Anne Rabe (GERMANY)

Anne Rabe was born in 1986 in Wismar, in the north of the former GDR. She studied creative writing at the University of the Arts, Berlin. Her plays are performed throughout Germany; amongst other theatres, at the Schaubühne, Berlin. *Sunflower House* had a British premiere, and the first full production in English of any contemporary East German author. In Germany, the play raised considerable controversy due to its criticism of the post-unification situation in the north of the country. Rabe has also published poetry, short stories and essays. She was the recipient of the Kleist Award (2006) and the Schiller Memorial Award (2010). She lives in Berlin with her husband and children.

Harmful

always those roaring
trains in my
head. alarm bells
of the traffic lights, one
to eleven. yet again
green lingers in the
empty streets. go!
I will not go.

o.t.

das licht
fällt all zu oft auf
die fratzen,
die mich umgeben. dem drang
nach außen
wird nicht nachgegeben.
der puls durchdringt
den kopf.
der knall bleibt innen.
hält das skelett zusammen
und schweißt mich ein.
ach,
lass uns einander
wieder lieben,
wie wir es als kinder taten.

u.t. (untitled)

the light
too often highlights
the grimaces
that surround me. the urge
for the outside
won't be fulfilled.
the pulse pierces
the head.
the beat remains inside
holds the skeleton together
welds me to it.
ah,
let us
love each other
the way we did as children.

ende

und dort herum
die kindergreise.

aus den augen der mädchen
läuft der unbrauchbare samen
vieler jungen.

und die tränen klatschen
auf ihr haar,
wie der regen
auf die baumkronen.

und ungeschützt sind sie
und nass.

die junge frau a.

am tag sieht man sie
flüstern unter bäumen.

ihre lippen sind spröde
und ihr hals ist getrocknet.

die trüben augen können kaum
die jahresringe sehen
an denen sie die zukunft weissagt.

the end

in that place
children grow obsolete.

useless seeds
of many boys trickle down
from the eyes of girls.

and tears fall down
on your hair,
like the rain
upon the treetops.

and they are unprotected
and wet.

young mrs. a.

in the daytime you can hear
her whisper under the trees.

her lips are chapped
her throat dry.

the dull eyes can hardly see
the annual growth rings
which she uses to foretell the future

gestern wusch sie sich
noch die hände.
wohl zweimal.

ja,

ich bin ein einhorn.
ich bin eins
mit meinem horn.

steche der wahrheit
ins gesicht
und lache: lüge!

will sie nicht hören,
die worte,
die klingen wie chaos.

lüge.
alles lüge.
und ich mit einem horn.

she washed her hands
only yesterday.
seemingly twice.

yes,

I am a unicorn.
I and my horn
are a single whole.

I sting the truth
in its face
and laugh: lie!

I don't want to hear
the words
that sound like chaos.

lie!
everything's a lie
and so am I, with my horn.

[In den Pausen zwischen den Bäumen: Schnee]

In den Pausen zwischen den Bäumen: Schnee
in den Räumen zwischen den Worten: Schnee
in den Mulden zwischen den Häusern: Schnee
in den Gärten zwischen den Zäunen: Schnee
und kalt
in den Teichen zwischen den Kneipen: Schnee
in den Löchern zwischen den Eichen: Schnee
in den Träumen zwischen den Feldern: Schnee
in den Tellern und Falten: Schnee

Ilma Rakusa (SWITZERLAND)

Ilma Rakusa was born in 1946 in Slovakia, and grew up in Budapest, Ljubljana and Trieste. In 1951 she moved with her parents to Zurich. From 1965 to 1971 she studied Slavic and Romance languages in Zurich, Paris and St. Petersburg. In 1977 she made her debut with the poetry collection, *As in Winter.* Since then, she has published a number of further collections, including *One Stroke through Everything* (Suhrkamp, 1997), and books of prose, including essays. Rakusa translates poetry from Russian, Serbo-Croatian, Hungarian and French, and has published articles in *Neue Zürcher Zeitung* and in *Die Zeit.* She has also been teaching Eastern European literature in Swiss universities. She is a member of the German Academy for Language and Literature, and lives in Zurich.

[In the spaces between the trees, snow]

In the spaces between the trees: snow
in the breaks between the words: snow
in the hollows between the houses: snow
in the gardens between the fences: snow
and cold
in the ponds between the pubs: snow
in the pits between the oaks: snow
in the dreams between the fields: snow
on the plates and in the folds: snow

[Vom Schlaf reden]

Vom Schlaf reden
vom Wachliegen nachts
den obskuren Zäsuren
wenn der Fuchs schreit
wenn die Ambulanz pfeift
wenn der Schweiß erkaltet
wenn das Kind nebenan seine eigene
Einsamkeit probt und tonlos
das Telefon blinkt wozu so grün

Sommer

Sommer ist:
wenn das Zimmer bei halbgeschlossenen
Jalousien vor sich hin dämmert,
wenn eine einsame Fliege brummend
das Freie sucht und nicht findet,
wenn draussen Zikaden zirpen
bei brütender Hitze, während über
die Fliesen Lichthasen huschen,
zitternd weisse Geschöpfe,
und Vasen, Töpfe, Krüge als
Stilleben gänzlich ruhen.

[Talking about sleep]

Talking about sleep
about lying awake all night
with blurry breaks
when the fox screams
when the ambulance hoots
when sweat grows cold
when the child next door rehearses
his own loneliness and the telephone
flashes tonelessly – why so green?

Summer

Summer is:
when the room with semi-closed blinds
dozes off on its own
when a lonesome buzzing fly
searches for freedom but can't find it
when cicadas chirp outside
in sweltering heat while transparent rabbits
scurry across the tiles,
trembling white creatures,
when vases, pots and jars never move
as in a still life painting.

Koffer

Koffer sind Koffer
sind Abschied
sind Leder
sind Fass-mal-an
sind Pack-mich-voll
und wieder aus
sind Bäuche
sind Häuschen
sind Wir-ziehen-von-
hier-nach-dort
und von dort
ach ja
nach weiter

[Schau die Sonne im Strauch]

Schau die Sonne im Strauch
schau den Wind im Geäst
schau den Vogel im Baum
schau den Schatten im Gras
schau
schau den Bleistift im Buch
schau das Wasser im Glas
schau die Freude im Raum
schau mich an schau

Suitcases

Suitcases are suitcases
are partings
are leather
are hold-my-handle
are pack-me-full
and then unpack
are bellies
are little cottages
are what-we-move-
from-here-to-there
and from there
oh yes
even farther

[Watch the sun in the bush]

Watch the sun in the bush
watch the shadows in the grass
watch the wind in wild broom
watch the bird in the tree
watch
watch the pencil in the book
watch the water in the glass
watch the joy in the room
watch me watch

In tiefer Nacht

In tiefer Nacht liege ich in mir
Und der Planet stößt an meine Nase
Eiseskalt, draußen wütet der Westwind. In mir
Ist ein Ozean, der aus Millionen
Korpuskeln Sesamschließdich
Besteht und diese Millionen
Durchfluten mich, daweil
Ich da liege in meiner Behaustheit
Blöd und träge lächle.
Auf dem Rücken lieg ich
Auf dem Bauch, wenn
Der Traumsturm mich wendet

Robert Schindel (AUSTRIA)

Robert Schindel was born in 1944 in Bad Hall, Austria, into a Jewish family. His father perished in the concentration camp in Dachau; his mother survived the camps and was reunited with her son in 1945. Schindel studied philosophy and law in Vienna, and worked as a bookseller. His first novel, *Cassandra,* was published in 1970. Since 1986 he has worked as a free-lance writer. He has published nine collections of poems, the latest being *My Clickable Lifespan* (2008), and three novels. He was awarded the Erich Fried Prize in 1993, the Eduard Mörike Prize in 2000 and the Heinrich Mann Prize in 2014.

In the Dead of Night

In the dead of night I lie inside myself
And the planet collides with my nose
Ice cold outside, the westerly wind rages. Inside me
An ocean consisting of millions of
Corpuscles – Sesame, close! –
And these millions are
Floating inside me
As I lie in my sanctuary
Smiling a silly and lazy smile
Lie on my back or
On my belly while
The dream storm stirs me

Dumme Liebe 2

Einerlei gefletschtes Innesein
Das schwimmt, das hält sich
Am Ununterbrochenen fest

Du. Mein gemaserter Sinn
Du, marmorgekörpertes Scheinen
Ich. Eingesperrt in der Aussenheit
Schicke mein Wort. Schicke und schicke

Lieblied 18 (Zauberhafte Nacht)

Zauberhafte Nacht. Die Zwillinge
Über der Frankfurter Skyline. Ich
Eingewickelt im eigenen Atem
Suche in deinen Augenblicken
Mein fremdes Antlitz, doch es weht
Dein Atem vom Norden her
Verfängt sich unterm Hemd und
Zauberhafte Nacht

Kastor und Pollux
Eingesternt in den Ewigkeiten. Wir aber

Aber wir. Ach wir. Wir beide
Zuluste und zuleide

Dumb Love 2

Internal life's monotony revealed
It floats, clings to
What remains whole

You. My multi-faceted feeling
You, my shiny marble lookalike
I, trapped in the outside world
Send you my word. Keep sending it

Love Song 18 (Magical Night)

Magical night. Gemini, the twin stars,
Over the Frankfurt skyline.
Wrapped in my own breath, I
Search for my unknown face
In your glances but your breath
Comes from the north
Wafts between my shirt and the
Magical Night

Castor and Pollux
Stuck in the aeons. However, we

We, however. Oh, we. The two of us
In joy and sorrow.

Kleiner Versuch Todesorgel

Man könnte auch sagen
Schluck auf Schluck ist nicht Schluck auf Schluck
Schluck ist für sich, Schluck ist für sich

Man könnte auch sagen
Antwort auf Frage ist nicht Antwort auf Frage
Antwort ist für sich, Frage ist für sich

Man könnte auch sagen
Leben zum Tod ist nicht Leben zum Tod
Leben ist für sich, Tod ist für sich

Man könnte auch sagen
Man könnte auch sagen ist nicht man könnte auch sagen
Man könnte ist für sich, auch sagen ist für sich

Schluck auf Schluck
Antwort auf Frage
Leben zum Tod
Man könnte auch sagen

A Half-Hearted Attempt to Play the Dead Organ

One could also say
Sip by sip isn't sip by sip
A sip is one thing, the next sip another

One could also say
An answer to a question isn't an answer to a question
An answer is one thing, a question another

One could also say
Life till death isn't life till death
Life is one thing, death is another

One could also say
One could also say doesn't mean that one could say it
One could is one thing, saying it another

Sip by sip
An answer to a question
Life till death
One could also say

Im Hin und Her

Im Hin und Her
Wenn den Leuten die Wörter
Aus dem Mund fallen und jeweils
An Anderen was bewirken
Oder eben schon gar nicht

Kauere ich in der Windstille
Die Ohren fest an den Seitenteilen
Des Schädels und falls
Allmählich der Westwind anhebt
Bewegen sich meine Nüstern
Unwillkürlich und ich wende
Dem Wind den Rücken zu

Back and Forth

Back and forth
When people drop words
Out of their mouths each
Has an effect on the others
Or not at all

I crouch in the still air
Ears firmly to the sides
Of my skull and if
The westerly wind picks up
My nostrils will start moving
Involuntarily, and I'll turn
My back to the wind

[Am höchsten Gipfel der Worte]

Am höchsten Gipfel der Worte
werde ich einen Galgen errichten.
Daran wird baumeln:
Alles Geflüsterte.
Alles Sehnsüchtige.
Alles Versprochene.
Alles Erdenkliche und Erdachte.
Wohl formuliert

Peter Turrini (AUSTRIA)

Peter Turrini was born in Wolfsberg, Carinthia in 1944 into a family of Italian furniture makers. His first play was published in 1967. Since then, he has published many other plays and screenplays, as well as poems, novels and essays. His plays are performed worldwide. His first collection of poems, entitled *A Few Steps Back,* appeared in 1980; his second, *In the Name of Love,* in 1993. In 1981, he was awarded the Gerhard Hauptmann Prize. He lives in Vienna.

[Atop the Highest Peak of the Words]

Atop the highest peak of the words
I will erect a gallows.
The following will dangle from it:
All the whispered.
All the desired.
All the promised.
All the imaginable and imaginative.
Well drawn up.

[Du stürmst in das Zimmer]

Du stürmst in das Zimmer
und schreist
wie sehr du mich haßt.
Ich mich auch. Da wir uns einig sind:
Könnten wir uns nicht
ein bißchen näher kommen?

[Ein Blick auf dich]

Ein Blick auf dich
und ich seh so viel Schönheit
so viel Schüchternheit
so viel Ausgelassenenheit
so viel Mut.

Was werde ich erst sehen
wenn ich noch einen Blick riskiere?

[You burst into the room]

You burst into the room
screaming that
you really hate me.
I too hate myself. So we agree on that.
Can it bring us
a little closer?

[Looking at you]

One look at you –
and I see such beauty,
such shyness,
such exuberance,
such courage!

What will I see
if I risk another?

[Am Ende des Horizontes]

Am Ende des Horizontes
brennt ein Feuer.
Ich verständige sämtliche Feuerwehren
der Umgebung
und eile mit ihnen
an den Ort des Brandes.
Dort brennt kein Haus.
Kein Stadel, kein Strohhaufen.
Dort stehst du.
Du zeigst auf dein brennendes Herz
lächelst
und forderst mich auf
auch das meine zu entzünden.
Ich hätte ja genug
Feuerwehren mitgebracht.

[At the end of the horizon]

At the end of the horizon
a fire burns.
I contact the emergency services
in the region
and hurry with the fire engines
to the site of the conflagration.
There's no house burning.
No barn or pile of straw.
You stand there.
You point at your blazing heart
smiling
and challenge me to
set fire to mine.
I wonder if I've brought
enough engines.

[Wir werden der Nacht]

Wir werden der Nacht
eine offene Rose
entreißen.

Wir werden aus der Mauer
eine Handvoll Samen
holen.

Wir werden aus dem Schweigen
Purzelbäume
formen.

Wenn ich einen Termin frei habe.

[In the Night]

We'll wring
a blooming rose
from the night.

We'll get a handful
of seeds
out of the wall.

We'll form
somersaults
out of silence.

If ever I have spare time.

hamburg – berlin

der zug hielt mitten auf der strecke. draußen hörte
  man auf an der kurbel zu drehen: das land lag still
  wie ein bild vorm dritten schlag des auktionators.

ein dorf mit dem rücken zum tag. in gruppen die bäume
  mit dunklen kapuzen. rechteckige felder,
  die karten eines riesigen solitairespiels.

in der ferne nahmen zwei windräder
  eine probebohrung im himmel vor:
  gott hielt den atem an.

Jan Wagner (GERMANY)

Jan Wagner was born in Hamburg in 1971 and has been living in Berlin since 1995. A poet, essayist and translator, he studied English literature at the University of Hamburg, at Trinity College Dublin and at the Humboldt University of Berlin. His first collection of poems, *An Exploratory Drill in Heaven*, appeared in 2001; his latest, sixth collection, entitled *Rain Barrel Variations,* in 2014 (Hanser Verlag, Berlin). He has also published translations from Irish, English, and American poetry. With the poet Björn Kuhligk, he edited the anthology of new German-language poetry titled *Poetry of Today: 74 New Voices* (2003). In 2004, he was awarded the Anna Seghers Prize; in 2009, the Wilhelm Lehmann Prize; in 2011, the Hölderlin Prize of the city of Tübingen and the Kranichsteiner Literaturpreis.

hamburg – berlin

the train halted in the middle of the track. outside
    they'd stopped rotating the crank: the land lay still
    like a painting waiting for the auctioneer's third hammer blow.

a village with its back turned to the day. groups of trees
    wearing dark hoods. rectangular fields,
    the cards from a giant game of solitaire.

in the distance two windmills were drilling
    a test borehole in the sky;
    god held his breath.

giersch

nicht zu unterschätzen: der giersch
mit dem begehren schon im namen – darum
die blüten, die so schwebend weiß sind, keusch
wie ein tyrannentraum.

kehrt stets zurück wie eine alte schuld,
schickt seine kassiber
durchs dunkel unterm rasen, unterm feld,
bis irgendwo erneut ein weißes wider-

standsnest emporschießt. hinter der garage,
beim knirschenden kies, der kirsche: giersch
als schäumen, als gischt, der ohne ein geräusch

geschieht, bis hoch zum giebel kriecht, bis giersch
schier überall sprießt, im ganzen garten giersch
sich über giersch schiebt, ihn verschlingt mit nichts als giersch.

am straussee

september. der sommer zieht sich trotzig
zurück aus den pappeln, bunte fahnen schwenkend.

und wir auf dem steg – wie vergessen. am himmel
beginnt man den roten teppich zu entrollen.

goatweed

is not to be underestimated: goatweed, *
with desire already within its name – hence
its flowers, vaguely white, innocent and sweet
as a tyrant's dream.

it always comes back to haunt us like an old guilt,
sends its secret message
through the darkness beneath the lawn, beneath the field,
then up again somewhere, a white cluster of resistance

shoots up. behind the garage, over the crunching gravel,
by the cherry-tree: goatweed as a foam,
as a spray: creeps silently toward the gable,

sprouts up throughout the garden. goatweed
almost everywhere: goatweed crawling over goatweed,
engulfed in nothing but goatweed.

* *giersch, the German for 'goatweed', contains the word 'gier' meaning desire.*

on straussee

september. summer retreats reluctantly through
the row of poplars waving multi-coloured flags.

and we stand on the footbridge – like two of the
forgotten ones. in the sky they begin to unroll the red carpet.

die ente dort, den kopf unter wasser, flüstert
irgend jemand auf dem grund des sees

leise etwas zu das uns betrifft.

im sommer '99

die luft mit der dichte von carraramarmor:
eine frage der zeit, dann bräche der asphalt
zusammen unterm kreuzverhör der sonne.
am himmel suchte ein flugzeug das loch im blau.

während die welt sich sehnte nach den richtig
großen tragödien, saßen vor meinem fenster
die grillen an ihren winzigen nähmaschinen,
tastete ich in den schubladen meines schreibtischs
nach den abstecknadeln der worte.

in der stille des postamtes schob man
kühle weiße briefe über den schalter
wie konfessionen durch die trennwand des beichtstuhls.
die adressen sind noch zu schreiben.

the duck nearby dips her head under water
and whispers softly to someone at the bottom of the lake

something about us.

in the summer of '99

the air as dense as Carrara marble:
it was only a matter of time before the asphalt
would crack under pressure, cross-examined by
the sun. a plane was looking for a hole in the blue sky

while the world was longing for truly great
tragedies, crickets were sitting in front of
my window operating their tiny sewing machines
I was fumbling about in my desk drawer
for pins of words.

in the silence of the post office they pushed
cold white envelopes through the opening above the counter
like the sacrament through the grid of a confessional.
the addresses are still to be added.

kohlen

auf klappernden pritschenwagen durch die stadt
im spätsommerlicht – die nacht in kleinen stücken.

von kräftigen armen von einem keller in
den nächsten gelagert (von dem der erde in meinen),

schweigend, wissend, kalt: ein haufen
von schwarzen augen, die nicht blinzeln werden.

bis sie im feuer zu liegen kommen.
bis der uralte wald in ihnen zu sprechen beginnt.

coals

through the city on clattering flatbed lorries
at summer twilight – the night comes in small portions.

transported by strong arms from one cellar to
another to be stored (from the earth's to mine)

silent, knowing, cold: a heap
of black eyes that won't blink

until they end up in the fire.
until the ancient forest begins to speak through them.

Das Meer kennt kein Meer

das Meer kennt keine Tiefe
kein Blau kennt seine Wellen nicht
das Meer ist nicht stolz nicht
sanft und nicht bitter
schmeckt nicht den Wind nicht den Schaum
das Meer sieht keine Sonne
kein Land und kein Geröll
das Meer liebt nicht den Himmel
nicht den Mond
das Meer kennt sich nicht

Eva Christina Zeller (GERMANY)

Eva Christina Zeller was born in Ulm, Swabia, in 1960, and now lives in Tübingen. She studied philosophy, German literature, theatre and rhetoric in Berlin and Tübingen. In 1988 she worked as a lecturer at the University of Otago in Dunedin, New Zealand. At present she works as a freelance writer and radio journalist. She has published several collections of her poetry, the latest being *Love and Other Journeys* (2007).

The Sea Knows no Sea

the sea knows no depth
no blueness it doesn't know its waves
the sea isn't proud or
gentle or bitter
it doesn't taste the wind or the foam
the sea can't see the sun
or land or ruins
the sea doesn't love the sky
or the moon
the sea doesn't know itself

Hölderlin war nicht in Tübingen

Er ist nicht hier gewesen
er hatte hier nichts zu finden

Er schaute nicht aus dem Fenster
er las keine Bücher
er zog nichts nach sich
er hinterblieb nicht

Er wankte nicht über die Straße
er zog keinen Hut
er ging nicht über die Brücke
er legte seinen Arm um nichts

Er ist nicht hier gewesen
er lebte um keinen Preis
er lebte woanders

alles nur bilder:

der körper unter dem leintuch
wie er kleiner wird

die hand leichter
wie sich alles zurückzieht

verbirgt wie die gegenstände
zu sprechen beginnen

Hölderlin Never Lived in Tübingen

He never came here
he had nothing here to look for

He didn't peep out the windows
he didn't read any books
he made no connections
he has no posthumous presence

He did not plod along these streets
he didn't take his hat off
he never crossed the bridge
he never put his arm around anything

He never came here
he'd never choose to stay here
he lived somewhere else

Everything's Just Pictures:

the body under the sheet
as it is shrinking

the hand gets lighter
as it retreats from everything

hides the objects
as they begin to speak

die brille verwaist
die schuhe plötzlich herrenlos

selbst die amsel vor dem fenster
singt dringlicher

nur das kinntuch
spricht von arbeit

die stimmen zu laut
als wenn er sie noch hörte

selbst der brustkorb
könnte sich noch bewegen

sagt unser auge
das getäuscht werden will

die erinnerung ist ein geisterfahrer

der fährt dir im dunkeln entgegen
er sieht dich nicht
du siehst nur ein licht
das dich blendet
umrisse schwimmen davon
vielleicht bist du der geisterfahrer
den du nicht erkennst

the orphaned spectacles
the shoes abandoned suddenly

even the blackbird outside the window
sings urgent songs

only the chin cloth
speaks of working

the voices too loud
as if he could hear

even the chest
could still move

that's what our eyes say
they want to be deceived

Memory is a Ghost Rider

who drives towards you in the dark
he doesn't see you
you only see the light
that blinds you
the outlines vanish
maybe you're the ghost rider
you just don't recognise

umarmung

nachts deine arme
spüren im erwachen
erinnere mich dass es dich gibt
könnte auch ein engel sein
oder eine mutter
eine erinnerung an etwas
was es vielleicht nie gab
nur der abdruck in mir
des ersten wunsches der menschen
im mutterleib und in den höhlen
als sie pferde wisente mammuts malten
ihre hände hinterließen bunt für alle zeiten

EVA CHRISTINA ZELLER

Embrace

deep in the night I feel your arms
at the moment of awakening
this reminds me that you are here
could also be an angel
or a mother
a memory of something
that might never have existed
only a memory print in me
the first wish of those who dwelt
in the womb or in a cave
painting horses bison mammoths
and left their coloured handprints for all time

ACKNOWLEDGEMENTS

The editor and publisher are grateful to the following copyright holders for permission to include original German-language poems in this volume. Where poems are previously uncollected in book form, copyright shall be understood to rest with the author. Copyright that rests with publishers or estates is acknowledged after the name of the author. Any errors or omissions in this list are entirely unintentional and the publisher shall undertake to make good any such errors or omissions in future editions.

Michael Augustin: 'Ortsgespräch Lübeck / Local Call, Lübeck' © Edition Temmen & Michael Augustin, 1993); other poems by permission of the author;

Nora Bossong: 'Geweihe / Antlers' and 'Rattenfänger / Ratcatcher' © Zu Klampen Verlag, Springe, 2007; 'Maria ad Naves / Maria ad Naves' © Hanser Verlag, Berlin, 2011; other poems by permission of the author;

Manfred Chobot: poems by permission of the author;

Daniela Danz: 'Stunde Null: Loop / Zero Hour: Loop' © Wallstein Verlag, Göttingen, 2014; 'Passage / Passage', 'Thin Red Line / Thin Red Line', 'Telepylos / Telepylos', 'Die Kamera im Dienst der Ethnologie / The Camera in the Service of Ethnology' © Wallstein Verlag, Göttingen, 2009;

Ludwig Fels: all poems © Jung und Jung, Salzburg, 2010

Brigitte Fuchs: all poems by permission of the author;

Durs Grünbein: all poems © Suhrkamp Verlag, 2006;
Annette Hagemann: all poems by permission of the author;

Ulla Hahn: all poems © Deutsche Verlags-Anstalt, München,
in der Verlagsgruppe Random House GmbH, 2013;

Felix Philipp Ingold: 'Ausgesungen / from Aftersong' © Rainer
Verlag, Berlin, 1993; [Hören auf das was nie] / [Listen to what
never] © Verlag Jutta Legueil, Stuttgart, 2000; other poems by
permission of the author;

Mathias Jeschke: 'Fahrt im Sommer / Summer Trip'; 'Kleines
Geläut / Small Bells' and 'Fahrt in die Endlichkeit / Journey in
the Finitude' © Rimbaud Verlag, Aachen, 2007; 'Unterwegs /
On the Way' © Edition AZUR, Dresden, 2010; 'Spiel zwischen
Erde und Himmel / Match between Earth and Heaven' by
permission of the author;

Uwe Kolbe: all poems by permission of the author;

Anton G. Leitner: 'Zu verkaufen / For Sale', 'Kleine Welt
Runde mit F. / A Short Round-the-World Trip with F.' and 'Die
Bojen flüstern / Buoys Whisper' © Lichtung Verlag GmbH,
Viechtach, 2006; 'Ersthelfer / First Aid' © Daedalus Verlag
Joachim Herbst e. K., Münster 2011; 'Herr Endlich sprintet /
Mr. Finally' © Anton G. Leitner, Weßling, 2006;

Sabine Naef: all poems © Edition Korrespondenzen, Wien, 2005;

Anne Rabe: all poems by permission of the author;

Ilma Rakusa: '[In den Pausen zwischen den Bäumen: Schnee] /
[In the spaces between the trees, snow]' © Suhrkamp Verlag,
1997; [Vom Schlaf reden] / Talking About Sleep' © Suhrkamp

ABOUT THE TRANSLATORS

ANATOLY KUDRYAVITSKY lives in Dublin, where he is the editor of *Shamrock Haiku Journal*. Between 2006 and 2009 he worked as a creative writing tutor for the Irish Writers' Centre. He has published three collections of his poetry, the latest being *Capering Moons* (Doghouse Books, 2011), and three novels (the latest title is *DisUNITY*, Glagoslav, 2013). His anthology of Russian poetry in English translation, *A Night in the Nabokov Hotel* (Dedalus Press) appeared in 2006. He has also published English translations of the poetry of Tomas Tranströmer, Miron Białoszewski and a number of others.

YULIA KUDRYAVITSKAYA is based in Berlin where she is studying history and English and German languages at the Freie Universität Berlin. Her German-language haiku appeared in *Shamrock*, and won Honourable Mention in the World Haiku Association Junior Haiku Contest 2008. Her translations from German-language poetry have appeared in *Hayden's Ferry Review*, *The Wolf*, *Two Lines*, *The Construction Magazine*, *Plume* and on *lyrikline.org*. Her German translations of seven poems by Anatoly Kudryavitsky have been published in the online edition of *Das Gedicht*. She is the daughter of Anatoly Kudryavitsky.

Dedalus Press

Established in 1985, and named for James
Joyce's literary alter ego, the Dedalus Press
is one of Ireland's longest running
and best-known literary imprints.

For more information,
visit **www.dedaluspress.com**.

*"One of the most outward-looking
poetry presses in Ireland and the UK"*
—UNESCO.org